CROLITAN UN

Leeds Metropolitan University

17 0173997 2

Rural landscapes in Europe: *principles for creation and management*

by Sébastien Giorgis
France

Council of Europe
Conseil de l'Europe

Steering Committee for the Conservation and Management of the Environment and Natural Habitats
Planning and Management Series, No. 3 – Strasbourg 1995

Artwork and cover page: Bernadette Legrand

Illustrations: Denis Lacaille (Agence Paysages – Avignon)

Photographs: Administration des eaux et forêts, Luxemburg – Tzontcho BALKANDGIEN, Bulgaria – Centre méditerranéen de l'environnement, France – Coopérative laitière de Beaufort, France – Correia DA CUNHA, Portugal – Culterra Bern, Switzerland – Sébastien GIORGIS, France – Mirko HAIN, Czech Republic – Arpad KAKONYI, Hungary – Jeny KARK, Poland – Maison de la Grèce, Paris – Vincent MOTTE, France – Michèle MOREAU, France – M. A. NOIRFALISE, Belgium – Office du tourisme autrichien, Paris – M. C. PAPASTAVROS, Cyprus – Geoffrey PEARSON, United Kingdom – Claudine SEYFRIED, France – Kreis SOEST, Germany – Marcel VERNOOY, Netherlands.

LEEDS METROPOLITAN
UNIVERSITY LIBRARY
1701739972
E7-B ✓
588515   25/6/97
578.97
333.76094 S/0
(4)

This publication concludes the work accomplished by the Group of Specialists "Countryside, Wildlife and Landscape" between 1992 and 1994 under the auspices of the Environment Conservation and Management Division of the Council of Europe. The group was chaired by Mr José CORREIA DA CUNHA (Portugal). The other members were: Mrs Aulikki ALANEN (Finland), Mr Régis AMBROISE (France), Mr Kifayet DEMIR (Turkey), Mr Frank ERASMY (Luxemburg), Mr Michael FASEL (Liechtenstein), Mrs Dr Gerda FUTTERLIEB (Germany), Dr Johann GEPP (Austria), Mrs Rayna HARDALOVA (Bulgaria), Mr Hanno HENKE (Germany), Mr Arpad KAKONYI (Hungary), Dr Edwin LANFRANCO (Malta), Mr Hannu LUOTONEN (Finland), Mr Christodoulos MAVROVITIS (Greece), Mr Claudio MENICUCCI (San Marino), Professor Albert NOIRFALISE (Belgium), Mr Costas PAPASTAVROS (Cyprus), Mr Geoffrey PEARSON (United Kingdom), Mr Juha PYKALA (Finland), Dr Milan RUZICKA (Slovakia), Professor Lech RYSZKOWSKI (Poland), Mr Jean-Marie SINNE (Luxemburg), Mr Marcel VERNOOY (The Netherlands), Mr Daniel ZÜRCHER (Switzerland). The text describing examples of landscape management were drafted by members of the group.

Secretarial services were provided by Mr Jean-Pierre RIBAUT, Mr Hector HACOURT, Mrs Marie-Aude L'HYVER-YESOU and Mrs Françoise BAUER of the Environment and Conservation and Management Division.

Scientific aspect: Anouk ARNAL, Agricultural Engineer – Pierre FRAPA, Naturalist.

Council of Europe Publishing
F-67075 Strasbourg Cedex

ISBN 92-871-2757-3 ✓
© Council of Europe, 1995
Printed in Germany

Document published with the financial assistance of the Ministry of the Environment, France, Landscape Office.

contents

Landscapes form the face of the earth. They express the ongoing relationship between mankind and the environment.

Nature and culture combine in a constantly shifting pattern. The landscape is built and shaped day by day on the traces left by history.

In order to manage the landscape, we need to discover how it came to be as it is, by looking first at the geomorphological structure and then at all the determining physical and ecological factors.

We also have to rediscover the traces of the original ecosystems which previous generations have transformed, adapted and shaped, leaving behind evidence of their genius, or of their mistakes, as the case may be.

In addition to the objective approach of the ecologist or historian, sensitive perception can tell us much about the landscape. Our appreciation of it is largely subjective and involves value judgements. The future of European landscapes calls for a wide-ranging debate founded on ecological, economic and cultural values.

In these times of profound change, the future of rural landscapes in Europe will be decided by planners seeking balanced compromise between economic development and nature. The countryside was created, tended and used as living space by the rural community.
Farming and timber production were for a long time the principal activities. Relations between town and country are today undergoing a change: in addition to supplying farm produce, the rural community is turning its hand to providing recreation and services for towndwellers.
This change is making its mark on the landscape, and transforming it.
How to accomplish this change successfully in terms of quality is one of the issues Europe must today decide.

The wealth and variety of Europe's landscapes, combined with the productive stockpile of experimental schemes, procedures and operations of various kinds conducted in all countries of the continent, have prompted the Council of Europe to produce this handbook in the expectation that each country will thus benefit from the others' experience.

It is intended as a source of ideas for everybody involved in fashioning tomorrow's rural landscape: elected representatives, people with a professional interest in agriculture, forestry and planning, permanent and occasional residents, students and teachers. In this way, the landscapes which our generation creates in Europe will be a source of inspiration for those who come after us.

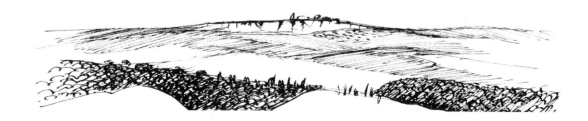

Europe's treasure trove of landscapes

"Four thousand years ago, Europe consisted largely of forests and marshes. Today it is a man-made garden, and the reason why people have become so fond of this garden is that they see it as the very image of their country, its physical characteristics."
René Dubos – 1972

Maison de la Grèce – Paris

Vincent Motte – France

Miko Hain – Czech Republic

Claudine Seyfried – France

Michèle Moreau – France

a mosaic of landscapes

Vincent Motte – France

Claudine Seyfried – France

Office du tourisme autrichien – Paris

Jerzy Kark – Poland

Ad. des eaux et forêts – Luxemburg

a cultural heritage

From the wide open moorlands and heathlands of the granite masses of Atlantic Europe to the rustic landscapes of the English Downs and the Carpathians;
from the stone-age bocage of the Celts to the gigantic stairways which score the Mediterranean uplands with low dry stone walls;
from the endless open spaces of the Ukrainian cereal-growing plains to the small enclosures separated by tall hedgerows in England and Normandy,
or to the steep meadows of the Alps; from the steppes of Hungary or the Caspian Sea to the verdant marshlands of Biebra in Poland;
Europe boasts an infinite variety of landscapes which are the bedrock
of each region and its inhabitants, bearing witness to their culture, their history and their know-how. By its beauty and its originality, the landscape is for everyone a point of reference, a source of happiness and an object of pride.

Our landscapes provide us with our first co-ordinates, forge our sensibilities and establish our aesthetic criteria. We appreciate them
with our feelings before apprehending them intellectually.
They express the diversity of our cultures and our mode of social and legal organisation and reflect each nation's creative ability
to adjust itself to the environment and derive a sustainable livelihood from it.

This immense diversity is one of the treasured assets of our continent and a part of its cultural heritage that we must not allow to deteriorate into dreary uniformity.

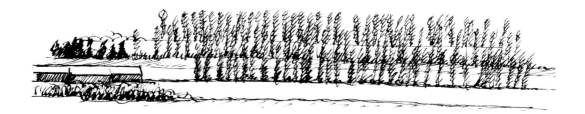

Tzontcho BALKANDGIEN – Bulgaria

A picturesque Bulgarian landscape

Man has lived there for centuries in perfect harmony with nature. The traditional livelihood is associated with forestry, mountain agriculture and livestock breeding.

The natural world itself and the region's material and spiritual culture offer outstanding opportunities for organising environmentally benign forms of tourism: nature study, rural pleasures, hunting etc.

The nature park shortly to be created will safeguard the wide diversity of wild plants and animals, the very numerous cultural monuments and the ethnographic heritage, and will provide local people with new resources in a well-tended, restful landscape.

the Rhodope Mountains: an attractive region

The beauty of their scenery, their biological richness and diversity and their unique atmosphere make the Rhodope Mountains irresistible.

It is a special and very specific world little known abroad, full of romanticism and a peacefulness that one no longer finds anywhere else. The countryside bears the imprint of honest farm labour.

Contact: Mrs Rayna Hardalova
Ministry of the Environment
67, W. Gladstone St 1000 Sofia – Bulgaria
Phone: + 359 2 661494

an ecological heritage

One of Europe's assets is its remarkable biological diversity which reflects the variety of geographical conditions that one encounters depending on whether the climate is oceanic, continental or Mediterranean, whether the substrate is granite or limestone, how high and how exposed the land is and whether water is scarce or abundant.

These factors are not alone sufficient to explain the complex mosaic of Europe's landscapes. They simply set the bounds of what is possible, the bounds within which human communities have left their mark. In order to live, they had to manage and organise the physical environment and work on it to create artificial, balanced or even improved habitats in which some animal and plant species, wild or tame, have thrived while others have been eliminated. The loss of biological diversity caused by the disappearance of natural countryside highlights the point at which human intervention should stop.

Each major type of man-made environment – hedgerow, openfield, marsh, terrace, forest, etc. – engenders an identifiable landscape, fosters particular skills and harbours those species that can adjust to it. The more these habitats have been transformed, the more they have come to depend on management and be vulnerable to dereliction or lack of upkeep. The polders are an extreme example.

The extent to which a community takes nature into consideration finds expression in its landscapes and their ability to sustain life in all its diversity

and over a long period of time. The earth is not simply a medium for human activity. It is a complex, living and fragile habitat which must be kept in good health.

an economic heritage

The countryside is the scene of essential economic activity:
farming, forestry, mining, etc.
The diversity of Europe's geographical conditions and the variety of the agrarian systems that have been devised, has made it possible
to develop a wide range of produce to meet the continent's vital needs.
But in addition to their directly productive functions,
rural landscapes represent an asset which every local development policy must take into account.
The identity which the landscape imparts contributes to
the inhabitants' quality of life and is largely responsible for their eagerness
to live and work locally.
Contractors and industrialists who care about their firm's image and
want their employees to have a congenial working environment are tending to
establish their headquarters in beautiful rural settings.
Tourists are beginning to turn their backs on the coastal
and mountain resorts where the landscape is spoiled by free-for-all development,
and seek peace and quiet in the authentic scenery of the European countryside.

Locating industries in the countryside creates jobs for the rural community,
stems depopulation and keeps desertification at bay.
All such development must comply with a planning policy in which care
for the landscape and the environment is paramount.
Rural tourism and crafts give farmers and other land
users the chance to earn a secondary income and so help them
to carry on fashioning and managing the landscape.

The urban world, which nowadays accounts for the major part of Europe's population,
benefits greatly from the maintenance and management
of the countryside by the rural community,
not least through the sheer pleasure that city dwellers derive
from beautiful landscapes.
The idea that city dwellers should make
a financial contribution towards the upkeep of the landscape
is making good headway.

**Landscapes are a part of every region's inheritance
and some regions are better endowed than others.
We must learn not to misuse it but to manage it
so that it will bear fruit.**

a precious asset under threat

The threats hanging over rural landscapes are of many kinds.
They range from certain unbridled forms of urban growth and tourism development to the often brutal technologies involved in road construction,
forestry and hydraulic engineering which fail to take account of the constituent elements of each particular site. Some regions suffer from
a proliferation of overhead cables, advertisement hoardings and chaotic signboards which rob the landscape of its character. Landscapes also lose
their substance when, through negligence or through lack of upkeep, the precious traces of the continuing history of a rural community are obliterated – features
such as age-old irrigation systems, stone walls, minor heritage items (wayside crosses, dove-cotes, wash-houses), authentic local housing,
not forgetting the vegetal structures, hedges in all their diversity, trees standing alone or planted in rows: such landmarks as these give identity to a region.

Changes in the rural economy and farming techniques sometimes tend to focus on productivity at the expense of quality – product quality, landscape quality
and the quality of the environment.

Developments which may well have a functional, utilitarian or economic justification nevertheless leave a bitter taste when they are not accompanied by a concern for quality in the present-day treatment of the physical or built environment.

The danger to Europe's rural landscape is twofold: overuse at one extreme, and dereliction at the other.

overuse

After the second world war, Europe succeeded in recovering its food independence and even began exporting its agricultural products worldwide.

The financial and human resources enrolled in the service of this policy and the power of the technologies applied, led to the belief
that it was possible to a large extent to shed the environmental and geographical contingencies which successive agrarian systems closely aligned
to rural conditions had taken on board, fashioning the principal features of the European landscapes.

Poorly planned land reallocation, as in Brittany in the 1970s, and the creation of plots of several hundred acres in the plains of central Europe, unjustified even
from the standpoint of heavy mechanisation, have brought about the destruction
of the intricate pattern of hedgerows, banks, stone walls, footpaths, thickets and rows of trees, and have rendered the landscape drab and sterile.

This *tabula rasa* landscape policy, combined with farming practices which make abundant use of synthetic weedkillers and fertilisers, contaminate the soil or eliminate crop rotation, is placing the whole environment at serious risk from soil erosion and pollution, ground water and surface water pollution, air pollution and loss of ecosystem and species diversity. The biological quality and the taste of some of the foods produced in these conditions are beginning to come under criticism from the consumers' organisations.

Similar technical problems concerning the environment and landscapes arise wherever woodlands are planted uniformly with species of short rotation, conifers especially, and where the timber crop is obtained by clear felling.

Paradoxically, some of the finest landscapes, including many that are protected, have suffered harm because their beauty, natural richness or cultural value has caused them to be overrun by tourists. It has reached the point in some Alpine resorts and on the Mediterranean coast where the landscape has become so blighted by tourism since the traditional rural activities were abandoned in favour of a tawdry jumble of infrastructures and facilities as to lose all the value they once had.

landscape management and erosion control in Westphalia

Soil in the rural district of Soest is very fertile. Because of intensive use, all landscape structures and the habitats they harboured have been wiped out.

The result has been a fall in productivity and an increase in water erosion, even on flat surfaces (fig.1).

The district authorities responsible for landscapes have developed a management policy aimed at establishing and conserving new landscape structures (hedges, grassland, lines and groups of trees, forests, terraces and walls) in co-operation with the local farmers.

The Benjes hedge is very appropriate in this context: cuttings and branches are piled to a height of about one metre in two rows, each three to four metres wide (fig.2), between which a hedge is formed naturally from seeds sown there by birds and wind dispersal.

This work is financed two-thirds from a federal nature conservation fund and one-third from a district fund for agriculture. Much of it is done by the local farmers.

Contact: Kreis Soest Umweltamt,
Abt. Natur und Landschaft Hoher Weg 1-3
D-59491 Soest – Germany
Phone: (02921) 300 – Fax: (02921) 302945

fig.1: soil erosion on flat surfaces in an area without landscape structures.

Kreis SOEST – Germany

fig.2: establishment of a Benjes hedge in an open field in combination with the planting of young oaks.

dereliction

While in some regions of Europe where the land is overused,
action is called for to allow the natural world
to regain its hold, other regions – upland regions especially –
suffer from farmland dereliction on a large scale.
The wasteland advances, villages die, landscapes, habitats and rural communities
vanish, and no-one has any alternative solution to propose.
The disappearance of the farming community
disrupts the social fabric.
Depopulation causes services, shops and schools to close down.
Life then becomes more difficult
for those who stay behind, jeopardising attempts
to revitalise the region.

On the mountains around the Mediterranean, for example,
the retaining walls
collapse where the terraces have been abandoned.
The landscape becomes blurred. An irreversible cycle of erosion,
wasteland formation and fire sets in. Rainwater is no longer retained and so flows
swiftly down into the valleys and causes flooding.

In other regions, planted forests are taking over from farmland
at such a rate as to smother the valley landscapes completely.

Villages are being choked and their attractiveness to tourists diminished,
while plants and animals which thrived
in the open spaces are disappearing.
The rural communities of Europe see abandonment as a sign of failure,
which adds to the discouragement
of the countryside's remaining inhabitants.

Some countries and regions have taken steps to curb this phenomenon.
The conservation farming measures proposed
by the European Union are a step in the same direction.
But if these measures to stimulate agriculture in the disadvantaged areas are not
accompanied by attempts to reduce
the incentives to produce more in intensively farmed areas, there is little hope of
halting this process of landscape simplification
where the only choice is between dereliction and overuse.

Culterra Bern – Switzerland

the traditional standard orchards of La Baroche.

rural landscapes safeguarded by the Swiss Fund for Landscape Protection (FSP)

In 1991, on the occasion of the 700th Anniversary of the Confederation, the Swiss Parliament set up a fund (the FSP) and placed 50 million Swiss francs at its disposal.

Its role is to provide support for innovative landscape protection and management projects and to reconstitute features which form part of the landscape. The fund has so far received 200 applications, of which 91 have already been processed by the FSP Commission and project committees. They include:

- *Restoration of the bisses (mountain streams diverted into small channels to irrigate meadows) in the canton of Valais;*
- *Mountain landscape management at Visperterminen (Valais) (including hayloft restoration);*
- *Measures to safeguard La Baroche (Jura), preserve orchards, keep hedges trim, reconstitute water courses and protect marshlands;*
- *Restoration of shingle roofs in the Fribourg and Vaud Prealps.*

Contact: Swiss Fund for Landscape Protection (FSP)
Hallwylstrasse 4 3003 Bern – Switzerland
Phone: 031/324 4989 – Fax: 031/322 9981

landscape management schemes in the Black Forest

The countryside of the Black Forest is a mosaic of woods, grasslands and fields, offering many habitats for plants and animals as well as a romantic setting. The decline of farming and the increase in afforestation are making the landscape monotonous and unattractive for tourism. At the same time, the quality of habitats for plants and animals is deteriorating (fig.1).

The nature conservation authorities, in co-operation with the agricultural authorities and with farmers, are therefore developing a management programme with the intention of saving this varied landscape.

Through special landscape conservation activities, suitable areas will be formed and cultivated that provide habitats for specific plants and animals (fig.2).

The maintenance of fields and grasslands for nature conservation purposes is a new source of income for farmers. Simultaneously, as landscape quality is being improved, there is increasing revenue from tourism as well.

fig.1: the forests in the mountains of the Black Forest are expanding. Farmland is used intensively, causing the loss of numerous wildlife habitats.

Kreis SOEST – Germany

fig.2: protection of diversity through conservation work in the southern Black Forest.

Contact: Ministerium für Umwelt – Baden - Württemberg ABT.
Ökologie und Naturschutz - Kernrplatz 9 – 70182 Stuttgart – Germany
Phone: (0711) 1260 – Fax: (0711) 1268 81

from conservation to landscape planning

from conservation . . .

Until quite recently, development and environment were thought to be irreconcilable.
The idea that the quality of the environment needed
to be maintained scarcely applied to the areas in which industrial agriculture,
urban growth and economic development were most profitable.
In reaction to this, nature and landscape protection and conservation procedures
were introduced to create zones for the preservation
of species diversity and landscape quality.
In nature reserves, regional parks and national parks, coercive measures valid in respect
of third parties were written into land use plans in order
to protect the natural assets and cultural features of the landscape.
The example of "Green Lungs"
was undertaken to preserve heritage in a region of 47 000 sq. km, located
in the north-east of Poland.
The land management plan for this area (production of healthy food,

eco-tourism as well as craft activities) is a pioneering effort in Europe.
An international extension of this initiative was signed by Poland, Belarus, Latvia,
Russia and Ukraine in 1992.

The Maastricht Declaration adopted at the EECONET Conference in November 1993
on conserving Europe's natural heritage
looks ahead to the implementation
of a European Biological and Landscape Diversity Strategy,
including a European Ecological Network,
as requested by the Convention on Biological Diversity (Rio de Janeiro, June 1992).

These instruments are concerned primarily with natural landscape
features and only marginally with cultural features.
Several European countries have developed specific instruments to protect the natural
beauty of landscapes
for their features of aesthetic or cultural interest.
In the United Kingdom, for example, areas of outstanding natural beauty (AONB)
total 2 700 000 hectares, but the inventory is not
backed up by any statutory restraints.
Germany has 5 000 areas under protection as landscapes
(Landschaftsschutzgebiete) totalling more than 6 million hectares.
The French law of 1930 is akin to the law on the protection of historic monuments in
that outstanding sites and landscapes are "listed".

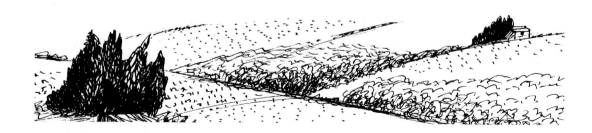

Landscape features, trees of outstanding interest, hedges,
alignments and groves may also be subject to particular protection measures,
as in Switzerland under the federal law on nature
conservation (Article 18*a-d*) and
the federal law on agriculture (Article 31*b*),
and in France under the "Landscape Law" of 8 January 1993.

Growing public concern has prompted the Unesco Heritage
Committee to consider including
the most remarkable cultural landscapes
in the World Heritage
List since 1992. These can include man-made rural landscapes.
In this way the decisive
contribution made by rural communities
to the progress of humankind is
duly acknowledged.
Protection of outstanding man-made landscapes should be seen as a means
of conserving places associated with
commemoration and inspiration. It is up to us to rediscover
the best of the values,
principles and know-how that went into their creation in order to improve
our management priorities for the future.

. . . to landscape planning

All these measures designed to protect the rarest and most vulnerable areas,
are of the utmost importance for conserving
biological diversity. However, they apply only to a limited percentage
of the European land area.
It would seem neither possible nor desirable to make them
apply to the whole of the countryside,
for fear of bringing all development to a halt, even though inaction may
sometimes be the wisest course.
In the busy, densely populated regions where the landscapes
are changing all the time, such instruments as these are ineffectual
and the issue for them is not one of protection
but one of planning: how to match landscape quality
with quality of life?

The landscapes with which we concern ourselves must result
from a global design and not simply from disorderly development,
the product of whatever power struggles
may be in progress between the parties involved.

There is no question of proposing
a single "model landscape",
since this would be inconsistent with the need for landscape diversity.

But it is possible to propose four fundamental principles which anyone responsible for creating and managing a contemporary quality landscape
would be invited to abide by; these are:

- Respect for regional identity and the right to enjoy beauty.
  Every society is entitled to express its character, its genius and
  its idea of what is beautiful, and for this the landscape is
  one medium among others.

- Respect for life and preservation of landscape diversity.
  Natural resources must be so managed as to enable present and
  future generations alike to make a living. Advocacy of sustainable
  development is therefore essential.

- Development of solidarity.
  Demands for space, quality of life and food supplies must be taken
  into account and shared among all sections of the community:
  productive landscapes accessible to all are therefore a necessity.

- Observance of democratic procedures.
  The landscape is everyone's concern. The standard of partnership,
  negotiating capacity and interchange among the social groups
  which create, manage and use the landscape will show in its quality.

Geoffrey PEARSON – United Kingdom

planning and development
in the Cairngorms

For many years, areas of high natural heritage value have been protected in the Cairngorms mountain area by a series of national and international designations. These have always covered a specific tract or site of high natural heritage interest.

The recent formation of a Partnership Board to co-ordinate the management of the Cairngorms area is a departure from this sectoral approach. The Partnership Board is made up of representatives from national and local government, voluntary organisations and sectoral bodies. It recognises that the present and future pressures faced by the Cairngorms area can best be met by an integrated management strategy. This strategy is built up around the protection currently offered through natural heritage designations, but also acknowledges that the natural environment is irrevocably linked with human activity in the area. Thus the partnership and strategy are based on the two principles of environmental sustainability and the social and economic well-being of the local population.

The partnership will draw up a management strategy to integrate activities in the area within a shared goal of achieving this underlying principle. It recognises that the overall protection and enhancement of the area and its precious natural heritage are best met through an holistic approach in which the impact of all factors (for example, tourism, local housing, employment) are taken into account.

As a voluntary grouping, the partnership is able to draw on the experience, expertise and finance of its partner bodies, influencing the way in which the area is managed. It represents a movement away from reliance on the protection of individual sites to the voluntary management of the wider area, caring for the general environment and landscape, and the people within it, as well as the specific areas of high natural heritage interest.

Contact: Mr Geoffrey Pearson
The Scottish Office Environment Department
Room 6/51, New St Andrew's House
Edinburgh EH1 3TG – GB
Phone: 44 131/244 4068 – Fax: 44 131/244 4071

Supraregional territorial system of ecological problems

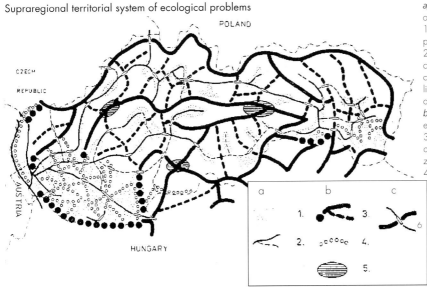

a) Territorial system of ecological stress factors:
1. Regions of ecological problems.
2. Main and secondary corridors of stress factors – concurrently barriers in the links of the territorial system of ecological stability.
b) Territorial system of ecological stability:
3. Main and secondary axes of ecologically more stable zones (belts).
4. Axes of more stable but comparatively isolated zones.
5. Main ecological nodes.
c) Meeting points of the territorial systems:
6. Position of bridges necessary for linking the more stable zones.

landscape ecological planning

Landscape ecological planning is one of the most important aspects of landscape ecology research and is developing due to the increasing problems in the interaction between society and the natural environment.

In Slovakia, the theory and methodologies of landscape ecological planning (Landep) have been developed over the last three decades as a specific form of complex landscape ecological investigations.

Landep is a system of applied scientific methods aimed at obtaining a new quality of knowledge by means of landscape ecological synthesis (based on typification) and the subsequent attribution of ecological value and functions to the landscape. The results obtained in the form of ecological proposals are used directly in practice.

Finding the most suitable locations of planned socio-economic activities in the landscape from the standpoint of landscape ecology may mean choosing the "lesser evil", that is places where a given activity will cause least disturbance to the natural conditions .

This is motivated by an effort to preserve the "life" of the landscape in terms of harmony, economy and ecology.

Contact: Dr Milan Ruzicka
Institute of Landscape Ecology
Slovak Academy of Sciences Akademicka 2 SR
949 01 Nitra – Slovak Republic
Phone: 42/87 356 02 – Fax: 42/87 356 08

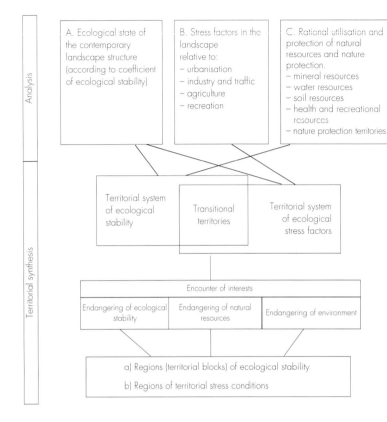

Analysis

A. Ecological state of the contemporary landscape structure (according to coefficient of ecological stability)

B. Stress factors in the landscape relative to:
– urbanisation
– industry and traffic
– agriculture
– recreation

C. Rational utilisation and protection of natural resources and nature protection.
– mineral resources
– water resources
– soil resources
– health and recreational resources
– nature protection territories

Territorial synthesis

Territorial system of ecological stability

Transitional territories

Territorial system of ecological stress factors

Encounter of interests

Endangering of ecological stability

Endangering of natural resources

Endangering of environment

a) Regions (territorial blocks) of ecological stability
b) Regions of territorial stress conditions

the general ecological model

The main objective is to make a substantial contribution to the process of ecologically sound landscape management. The ultimate goal of this endeavour is to create the preconditions for the community's overall development and to improve its standard of living with ecological welfare as the criterion of accomplishment.

The generation of ecological data is based on determining the ecological conditions that are necessary for managing the landscape, discerning the ecological problems of present-day management and proposing an ecologically optimal landscape management method.

The objective of this general ecological model stage was to make a survey of spatial differentiation of the major ecological problems of the country to the scale of 1: 500 000.

In the synthesis, regional ecological problems are divided into ecologically stable areas, environmental stress factors and factors endangering the ecological stability of the landscape, the natural resources and the environment. This result should serve as a basic foundation for a different approach to landscape management in other regions.

Contact: Dr Ladislav Miklos
Institute of Landscape Ecology
Slovak Academy of Science
Stefanikova 3 SR - 84199 Bratislava – Slovak Republic
Phone: 42/74 938 82 – Fax: 42/74 945 08

M. C. PAPASTAVROS – Cyprus

Terraces help to combat erosion and provide space in which to plant new crops

integrated rural development (IRD): the Pitsilia region

The Pitsilia region lies on the south-eastern side of the Troodos Mountain Range. It is one of a system of 29 agricultural regions of Cyprus and encompasses zones in the 600 to 1800 metre altitude range including 49 villages with a population of 21 000. The total surface area is 60 000 hectares. The Pitsilia project started as a pioneering project, its primary aims being: to improve the living standards and the quality of life of the people of the area through productive and socially useful investments; to develop and utilise the region's productive resources; to increase the Gross National Product; to conserve the natural and man-made environment.

After relevant studies of development potential in the context of the various physical, economic and social characteristics of the region, detailed techno-economic studies were made of the schemes included in the project.

The investments were concerned with production (89% of the total), social measures (9%) and institutions (2%). This allocation and the priority given to the productive sector mainly reflects the need to justify the development project on economic grounds.

Contact: Mr C Papastavros,
Ministry of Agriculture and Natural Resources,
Nicosia – Cyprus
Phone: 357/302586

guiding principles for landscape management

respect for regional identity and the right to enjoy beauty

Each landscape has a visage with features of its own.
Lines and points and surfaces form the shapes which make it unique,
unlike any other. Each has its own colours and its own mix of plant life and minerals.
The proportion and distribution of spaces
which are empty (grassland, areas under crops, moors and heaths)
and those which are not (woodlands, forests, orchards, etc.) lend each one its
particular feel and atmosphere.
The shape or form, the materials and the setting of the built environment all
help to situate the landscape in time and space.

How the landscape is organised depends on the pattern of the land: a patchwork of
tiny plots, long narrow strips or large acreages.
Distinctive forms and shapes give it structure: dark, serried lines of cypress trees
forming windbreaks, majestic alignments of tall trees alongside roads or canals, trees
which stand out at a crossroads or a dense labyrinth of hedgerows.

Some of these forms and shapes are extremely long-lived, going back thousands of years. They are the landscape's principal structure and framework:
valleys with rivers flowing through them, certain lines of communication, the location of villages and the orientation of land plots.
Others are of average longevity, measured in centuries. These include hedges, polders and tree alignments.
Others are measured in decades: the ratio of cultivated
to forested land. Then again some are ephemeral, like a field of flowering rape.

A landscape's identity is expressed by these characteristic features. It is rooted in time. It fashions our sensibility, expresses our culture and nurtures
our system of representation.

Working on a landscape, modifying it, and introducing a new development into it
are activities that presuppose an analytical faculty and a keen
understanding of this formal structure, this landscape geometry, and the ability to take account of the features that give it identity and their order of importance.
Also required is an understanding of the phenomena of individual
or collective perception associated with individual experience
or with culture, with the images fashioned by artists, described by writers,
sung by musicians and set in the scenery by landscape artists.

Gardening and agronomy always went hand-in-hand until quite recently, the garden being regarded as the place where our vision of and relationship to nature

and the broad landscape crystallises, and where formal models are tested and fabricated before being applied to the broad landscape, whereas the latter supplies the imaginations of garden designers with its inventions.

Through its gardens and through its landscapes, every society must be able to express its idea of what is beautiful, its cultural and aesthetic values.

some lines of action

◆ Compiling an inventory of each region's landscape units.

◆ Analysing the driving forces that determine the specific characteristics of the landscape.

◆ Analysing the structures and reference forms specific to each unit, and establishing an order of importance.

◆ Protecting and consolidating the enduring landscape structures.

◆ Restoring and reviving minor rural heritage items, gardens and vernacular architecture, and making those responsible for managing these assets aware of their importance.

◆ Compiling an inventory of representations: paintings, etchings, literary descriptions, photographs.

◆ Reducing the visual pollution that degrades the landscape (hoardings and signboards, overhead networks, messy building development, etc.).

◆ Promoting the development of an art form that expresses contemporary landscape trends.

respect for life and preservation of landscape diversity

The quality of the water and soil and the richness of the flora and fauna are fundamental considerations when judging the quality of a landscape.

They are closely interdependent: a hedge or a tree may be indispensable
for maintaining the hydraulic system, preventing soil
erosion or preserving biological diversity.
Constant attention must be given to making interests converge. Landscape design must enhance all the ecological interactions at work
in a site or habitat while at the same time making it attractive.

water: quality, economics and enjoyment

Water, the source of life for plants, animals and human beings, is also an energy source, a medium of communication
between regions and countries, and a source of enjoyment.
To enable all these functions to develop, people have at all times
endeavoured to interfere with the water's natural course,
derive benefit from it and limit the dangers it causes. This involves draining, irrigating, storing and distributing water and carrying out engineering works.

The landscape expresses the time-honoured human concern for the way water flows across the land.

It reflects the ingenuity of communities which succeeded in solving the problems
of water management in regions that were climatically
and geographically very different.

Water is one of the main structural features of the landscape: waterside woodlands
mark out its course in the valleys with a broad stroke,
the decisive lines drawn by irrigation or drainage channels determine
the lie of the land, and reservoirs
which may or may not be visible (lakes, dams, underwater streams,
ground water bodies, etc.) also make their impact felt.

Any action to modify this framework calls for more than just technical skills.
It needs a humanist outlook, a feeling for history
and geography and an understanding of the way in which people interact with nature
and relate to each other.

Considered interference with water can have adverse effects downstream or later in
time. Inadequate management or excessive pumping
in the underground reserves can have serious consequences: salinisation
may occur, as in parts of Hungary and Greece, springs may dry up
and deserts may form.
In the Paris basin, the pollutants used in intensive farming over the past three decades
will take some years to work their way through the chalky terrain into the ground
water; that they will do so one day is nonetheless inevitable.

Three guiding principles must be observed for sustainable water management in the landscape:

- Resource management: water is in limited supply; it must be used economically and managed in a manner that is both efficient and ecologically sound; this calls for an integrated approach.

- Maintaining water quality: pure water is crucial for a healthy environment: with a good knowledge of ecological processes, it is possible to preserve water quality without having to apply chemical treatments.

- Access to water: everyone should have access to water for enjoyment, in so far as this is consistent with the principle of wise use.

Global, integrated water management presupposes a concerted approach by everyone whose activity affects the landscape: local authorities, farmers, angling clubs, conservation organisations, environmental groups, local inhabitants, etc.

They must draw up the landscape plan together.

some lines of action

◆ Encouraging agrarian practices which are economical with water, cause little or no pollution and limit soil erosion.

◆ Developing landscape structures which help the process of water self-purification: restoring and consolidating riverside vegetation, developing wooded strips, grass verges and hedgerows.

◆ Preserving the visible presence of water instead of diverting it into concrete pipes or covering over watercourses and ditches.

◆ Protecting and restoring natural habitats associated with the presence of water, and avoiding the use of non-living materials on stream banks.

◆ Managing the recreational and educational potential of water in the countryside in a sustainable manner.

◆ Managing run-off channels correctly by keeping the stream bed in good order and controlling the extraction of materials (gravel).

◆ Preserving the built heritage associated with the presence and use of water (bridges, canals, springs, etc.) and guaranteeing the quality of new equipment.

Marcel VERNOOY – Netherland

managing a "natural" city: the example of Arnhem

The city of Arnhem (135 000 inhabitants), on the lower Rhine, has developed a nature conservation strategy in which green areas and waterways are allowed to blend naturally with the townscape to form green and blue "fingers".

A number of projects have been carried out: developing river forelands and natural areas, changing stony areas and lawns into semi-natural grasslands, planting trees, using indigenous instead of exotic species, discontinuing the use of chemical substitutes, etc.

Local residents are fully involved, both in the decision-making process and in the design of projects within their neighbourhood.

For this, Arnhem received the National Nature Conservation Award for Local Authorities in 1992.

Contact: Mr Marcel Vernooy and Hans Kampf
Ministry of Agriculture, Nature Management and
Fisheries – Posthose 20401
73 - 2500 EK's Gravenhage – Netherlands
Phone: 070/37 939 11 – Fax: 070/34 782 28

LEEDS METROPOLITAN UNIVERSITY LIBRARY

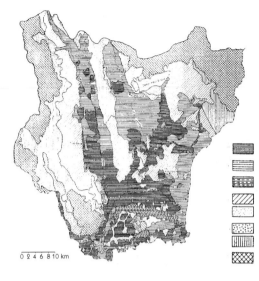

0 2 4 6 8 10 km

Schematic map of the geosystems of the east Slovakian Lowland

1 depressions
2 alluvial plains
3 undulating plains with flood-plain meanders
4 undulating plains on the loess
5 undulating plains of the sand dunes
6 hills with downsands
7 hills on the polygenous sediments
8 uplands

the east Slovakian lowland

The east Slovakian Lowland (ESL) comprises 200 660 ha of agricultural land, including 144 260 ha of arable land, with a mixture of natural conditions and specific potential for intensive agricultural production. The landscape, which shows the signs of intensive agricultural use, has changed as a result of improvements to its large-scale drainage system, which was in disharmony with the natural environment.

In landscape ecology, it is of the utmost importance to investigate and evaluate the substratum soil-relief-water complex, with regard to agricultural land use.

The most important present problems of ESL agriculture are: very heavy soils, clays and relief depressions on the same areas.

These properties cause long-term water-logging of farmland, mainly in the spring, when mechanised cultivation takes place; on the other hand, there is a lack of water in the subsequent growing period due to an extremely unfavourable water regime.

Suggestions for ecological optimisation resulted from further study of waterlogging and the possibilities of drainage, arability and present soil use. Those suggestions have proved decisive for the re-organisation of agriculture and land use generally.

Contact: Dr Milan Ruzicka
Institute of Landscape Ecology
Slovak Academy of Sciences Akademická 2 SR
949 01 Nitra – Slovak Republic
Phone: 42/87 356 02 – Fax: 42/87 356 08

Arpad KAKONYI – Hungary

lake Water Quality Improvement Programme: Lake Balaton

Lake Balaton is the biggest shallow lake in central Europe with an area of 572 sq. km. The average depth is only 3 metre, which is a crucial factor in ensuring water quality because the winds stir up the organic sediment. In the 1970s, human interference accelerated the entrophication process, making the water turbid and impairing the development of the fauna and flora. At that time, a series of measures was undertaken to improve water quality.

Over the whole catchment area, intensive livestock breeding has been discontinued. Around the lake, the development of sewerage systems and new treatment plants has been accelerated, applying the latest methods.

The Zala river and some other streams feed the lake, carrying 100 000 tons per year of suspended matter, municipal, industrial and agricultural waste.

Originally, the Kis-Balaton, a marshland acting as a natural filter-field, retained the river pollutants but at the turn of the century, due to failure to assess all the consequences, it was drained and the Zala polluted the lake directly. To ensure the restoration of the original function:
Phase I: 1981-89: area 18 sq km
– reservoir volume: 21 million m³
– cost 9 million United States dollars.
Phase II: 1990-99: area 51 Sq KMS
– reservoir volume: 64 million m³
– cost 65 million United States dollars of which 19 million dollars have been dispensed (1994).

The restoration of this wetland not only serves to improve water quality in the lake, but also provides valuable habitat for waterfowl and waders in accordance with the Ramsor Convention.

Contact: Mr Arpad Kakonyi
Kiskunság National Park Liszt F.19 H
6000 Kecskemet – Hungary
Phone: 36/76 482 611 – Fax: 36/76 481 074.

agro-ecological landscape park in Turew

The agro-ecological landscape park was founded in 1992 on an area of about 160 000 hectares in order to implement ecological guidelines for landscape management and provide examples of good farming practice. The area is located in the Wielkopolska region (western Poland) known as the "bread basket" of Poland. During the 1820s, Dezydery Chlapowski, a pioneer of modern Polish agriculture, planted an area of about 10 000 hectares with shelterbelts (rows of midfield trees or bushes) in order to improve the microclimatic conditions in adjoining fields and create livestock enclosures. The shelterbelt also provided timber and fuel, while improving the aesthetic image of the countryside.

The shelterbelts now have the following functions: control of erosion and diffusion of pollution; production of wood, fruit and seeds; maintenance of biological diversity.

Interfield meadow strips and shelterbelts act as barriers to the dispersal of chemical compounds from the cultivated fields. Ground water analyses show a considerable decrease in the concentration of certain chemicals, especially nitrates. These investigations point to the possibility of changing the ground water chemistry by manipulating the structure of watershed plant cover. Plant cover also decreases soil losses by water and wind erosion.

Contact: Mr Lech Ryszkowski
Research Centre for Agricultural and Forest Environment
Polish Academy of Sciences
Bukowska Street 19-60 809 Poznań – Poland
Phone: (0048) 61 - 475 605, (0048) 61 - 475 601

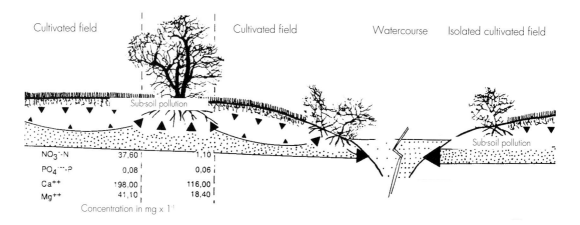

Hedge

Cultivated field   Cultivated field   Watercourse   Isolated cultivated field

Sub-soil pollution   Sub-soil pollution

NO_3^{-}-N	37,60	1,10
PO_4^{---}-P	0,08	0,06
Ca^{++}	198,00	116,00
Mg^{++}	41,10	18,40

Concentration in mg × 1^{-1}

soil: quality and economics

The soil is a highly complex medium created over thousands of years by the interplay of natural processes and human intervention.
The growth, health and quality of plants – and in particular the farm produce that we consume – depend on its equilibrium.
There are only limited amounts of this resource.
The soil cover is thin and precious. It is not a once-and-for-all gift. Generations of country folk created farmland by clearing the ground,
moving boulders and even, in the Mediterranean regions,
carrying soil on their backs from the valleys to the hillside terraces. They have constantly maintained, enriched and nurtured the soil in order to preserve its life-giving fertility.

Some agricultural practices nowadays treat the soil simply as an inert medium for crops fed solely with industrial chemical inputs.
With crop rotation processes becoming more simplified, organic fertilisers falling into disuse or being applied to excess and leguminous breaks virtually disappearing,
imbalances and deficiencies occur which in the long term
impair the soil's biological potential and lead to greater
recourse to chemical growth agents. The "disease" which has struck
the soil of the great cereal-growing plains of Ukraine illustrates this degenerative process.

Soils that are less rich in organic matter are still more sensitive to erosion by wind and water, phenomena which are amplified
when banks and terraces are allowed to disappear.
In southern Europe 25 million hectares are affected by erosion and are losing an average of 1,8 tons of soil per square kilometre every year.

A quality landscape plan must promote the long-term preservation of the organic quality of the soil to sustain its fertility.

A policy of limiting land overuse has beneficial effects on landscape quality in general, in so far as it makes for a more balanced
regional development of the regions and less dereliction and wasteland formation in the difficult regions.

some lines of action

◆ Maintaining, recreating and increasing the landscape structures, vegetable or mineral, which provide protection against erosion by wind or water.

◆ Encouraging farming practices which use and nurture the living properties of the soil: rotation cropping, balanced use of organic manure, reasonable mineral inputs, recycling of healthy organic wastes by composting.

◆ Promoting balanced utilisation of all productive land to prevent the soil being degraded by over-intensive use or dereliction.

Correia DA CUNHA – Portugal

Terraces for the production of port wine.

the human influence
on the Douro Valley landscape

The Douro Valley owes the diversity of its landscapes to the environmental and climatic features which very largely determine the economic activities for which the land is suitable.

The farming and forestry land uses differ from sector to sector and have little to do with geomorphological characteristics.

The terraces are indicative of the degree to which the human influence has been exerted on the landscape.

Planted on excessively steep hillsides without the aid of correctly constructed terraces, the vineyards of the Douro (the oldest defined wine-growing region in the world) are conducive to erosion and hinder soil formation.

Recent studies of the visual quality and vulnerability of the Douro landscape have prompted a campaign to mark out areas of comparable aesthetic value and draw up rules to regulate land use.

Contact: Mr Correia Da Cunha
Ministry of the Environment and Natural Resources and Ministry of Agriculture, Fisheries and Food
Rodrigo da Fonseca Street, 74-1°
Esq P-1200 Lisbon – Portugal
Phone: 351/1386 11 23 – Fax: 351/1 38 63 184

preservation of biological diversity

Rural landscapes contribute to biological diversity in three ways:

• By modifying environmental conditions, agriculture has created a range of new habitats to which certain species have become adapted, by quantitative selection and/or genetic specialisation.

• The vegetal structures and water systems which divide up the countryside form the habitat for many wild flora and fauna species.

• Domestic animals and crop-producing plants and trees obtained as a result of hybridisation, cross-breeding and selection, present a very rich genetic diversity.

Diversity of fauna, flora and natural habitats is one of the primary factors in the maintenance of natural balance. This diversity is endangered. In Europe, it is estimated that about 22% of higher plants, 52% of fish species and 42% of mammals are threatened with extinction. In absolute terms, the number of endangered invertebrate species is undoubtedly even higher. This is one of our most precious, non-renewable assets, and it is disappearing with the increased use of agricultural chemicals and the tendency to render landscapes monotonous and so reduce the habitat diversity they offer.

The landscape plan must maintain and develop the various life-sustaining processes and structures and give guidance as to the necessary management measures.

some lines of action

◆ Creating ecologically stable landscape structures on two levels:

international and national: the basis of this network consists of natural areas of major biological interest safeguarded by parks, reserves and various protected areas;

regional and local: here it is a case of ensuring continuity and liaison and providing migration corridors between the different natural features of the landscape: copses, hedges, waterside vegetation, etc.

◆ Supporting countryside stewardship by making remuneration conditional upon the signing of management agreements for areas and habitats totally dependent on such management: dry grasslands, wetlands.

◆ Recommending integrated pest control procedures which use the natural landscape structures as the habitat of the auxiliary fauna and minimise chemical treatments on crop and timber production plots.

◆ Developing institutions for the conservation of genetic varieties, promoting the rearing of rustic breeds, and demonstrating the potential economic value of this diversity.

transformation of the Hagmolenbeek into an ecological corridor

The Hagmolenbeek, a small waterway situated near Haaksbergen in the eastern part of the Netherlands, has been transformed into an essential link between two important heathland and forest areas. The slope on the southern side has been flattened to create a graduation of wetland habitats, and trees and shrubs have been planted. The work was carried out by the Ministry of Agriculture, Nature Management and Fisheries, in close co-operation with the local water board, Regge en Dinkel, and the national NGO Natuurmonumenten.

Within a few years, it is expected that the Hagmolenbeek will be recolonised and used as a migration route by, for example, kingfishers, badgers, butterflies and bats. As such, it is an example of the important function of ecological corridors as stepping stones within the ecological network of the Netherlands.

Contact: Mr Marcel Vernooy and Hans Kampf
Ministry of Agriculture, Nature Management and Fisheries
Posthose 20401
73 - 2500 EK's Gravenhage
Netherlands
Phone: 070/37 939 11
Fax: 070/34 782 28

core areas
Areas with (inter)nationally important ecosystems

Nature development areas
Areas offering perspectives for nature development

Dunes
Low-lying peatland and clay area
Higher (sandy) mounds and southern Limburg hills

Fluvial region (river forelands)

Large bodies of water
-mudflats

To be developed or reinforced

idem : concerning transboundary nature areas

Ecological corridors

the Zamagurie Region

The Zamagurie region is situated between the Tatra National Park and the Polish-Slovak border. It escaped damage during the period of agricultural collectivisation, and is a model of natural landscape structure and biological diversity.

It is proposed to save the existing ecological quality and restore the degraded landscapes. The most important "complexes" are: substratum relief (landslide risk), soil (stone content, structure with respect to cultivating), soil-relief-climate (erosion, transport of water and material on slopes), relief (accessibility for mechanisation), vegetation-animals (grassland, landscape greenery, avifauna, malacofauna). The synthesis of these "complexes" results in a map of biological quality of the landscape and establishes limits for desirable social activities in this region.

A region with a well preserved traditional historical structure of land use, Zamagurie should remain polyfunctional, serving the needs of agricultural production and recreation, while certain sites could serve as gene pools not only for autochthonous species, but also for cultivated plants and animals.
It has all the prerequisites to become a model territory for ecological husbandry under specific natural conditions with the emphasis on nature conservation.

Contact: Dr Milan Ruzicka
Institute of Landscape Ecology
Slovak Academy of Sciences Akademicka 2 SR
949 01 Nitra – Slovak Republic
Phone: 42/87 356 02 – Fax: 42/87 356 08

M. A. NOIRFALISE – Belgium

conservation policy in the Hautes Fagnes-Eifel nature park

The Hautes Fagnes-Eifel nature park extends over a total of 248 500 hectares (176 300 ha in Germany and 72 200 ha in Belgium). It includes a 4 000-hectare strict nature reserve of peat bogs and moorlands to which the European Diploma has been awarded.

In the rural area of the park (approximately 15 000 hectares):

Measures have to be taken to conserve and manage the valley floor grasslands with Narcissus pseudonarcissus and Meum athmanticum which the farmers have left untended.

There have been measures to safeguard the bocage character of the region, involving subsidies for the upkeep of the high beech hedges which surround the farm buildings and the hedgerows and the tall individual beech trees that mark the boundaries of the small hayfields.

Under the land use plan established before the park was created, it was compulsory to maintain the broadleaved forests, and conifer plantations were prohibited in the valley floor meadows. The most interesting natural habitats were designated as nature reserves or forest reserves.

A socio-economic survey is now in progress in an endeavour to consolidate the future of farming and agricultural employment in the region by developing selective tourism and arranging for the rural communities to look after the landscapes and natural habitats.

Contact: M. A. Noirfalise
Centre of Rural and Forest Ecology
Passage des Déportés 2-5800 Gembloux 9 – Belgium
Phone: 081/62 23 78

Deutsch-Belgischer Naturpark
Nordeifel-Hohes Venn
Monschauer Str. 12
D - 52076 Aachen – Germany

development of solidarity

productive landscapes . . .

Concern to increase food and timber production in order
to ensure independence or meet the needs of the world market is legitimate.
People need food, clothing, shelter and
the means of keeping warm.

The aim should be to use each region's potential
to the full and so ensure that wealth is better distributed, that fewer environmental
problems arise as a result of concentration, and that the cost of keeping
the land in good condition goes down.

The conclusion to be drawn from these principles where landscapes are concerned is
that regional diversity is desirable, as opposed
to uniformity and simplification resulting from the application
of models designed to produce maximum yields, where the emphasis is on
non-soil methods, monocultures, large-scale hydroponic or glasshouse cultivation.

The landscapes which we produce will reflect our economic choices.
The farmers who make it their business to preserve the olive bowers in which
the villages of the Alpilles nestle, almond orchards thick with
winter blossom, the distinctive terraces of the Douro valley, the dry stone walls around

English meadows, have frequently to battle against the tide of fashion,
a stand which, with hindsight, we now acknowledge as being perfectly right.
By associating the value of what they produce with the value of the landscape,
those farmers show genuine economic judgement
founded on cultural authenticity which the developers would do well to ponder. The "guarantee of origin" policy designed
to improve the relationship between product quality and landscape quality indicates
one line of action for associating a mode of production
more closely with a locality or region.

some lines of action

◆ Ensuring that each region's economic and ecological potential are balanced in a way which takes due account of the need for better distribution of wealth and of the environmental carrying capacity of the region.

◆ Supporting locally grown produce, certificates of quality and guarantees of origin, associating such measures with specifications giving prominence to agricultural practices that uphold landscape quality and preserve the environment.

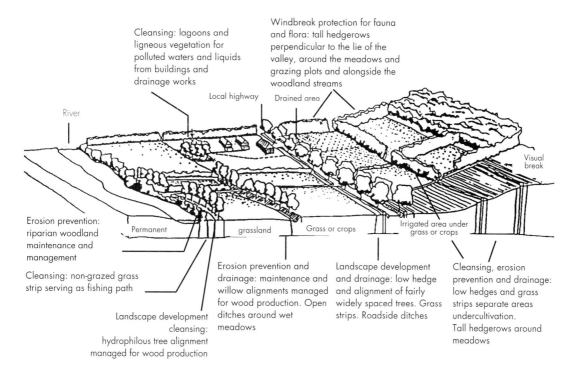

Cleansing: lagoons and ligneous vegetation for polluted waters and liquids from buildings and drainage works

Windbreak protection for fauna and flora: tall hedgerows perpendicular to the lie of the valley, around the meadows and grazing plots and alongside the woodland streams

Local highway

Drained area

River

Visual break

Erosion prevention: riparian woodland maintenance and management

Permanent

grassland

Grass or crops

Irrigated area under grass or crops

Cleansing: non-grazed grass strip serving as fishing path

Erosion prevention and drainage: maintenance and willow alignments managed for wood production. Open ditches around wet meadows

Landscape development and drainage: low hedge and alignment of fairly widely spaced trees. Grass strips. Roadside ditches

Cleansing, erosion prevention and drainage: low hedges and grass strips separate areas undercultivation. Tall hedgerows around meadows

Landscape development cleansing: hydrophilous tree alignment managed for wood production

Example: a landscape management scheme prepared for a sustainable development plan in the region of Segré.

plans for sustainable development

In France, plans for sustainable development have been introduced for the purpose of offering management contracts to any farmer wishing to change his present practices for a more sustainable form of agriculture. The idea is to harmonise the functions which the farmer performs in the production of food and industrial commodities, countryside stewardship (water, soil, biological diversity, landscape, etc.) and involvement in rural community life.

Financial support and partnership may come from various quarters depending on the produce offered or services rendered: EU, state, local or regional authorities, water agencies, tourism industry, fishing and field sports societies, conservation groups, etc.

This process is still at an experimental stage and is currently being tried out on 1 200 volunteer farm holdings by the Ministry of Agriculture and Fisheries.

Contact : Mademoiselle Dominique Legros
Ministère de l'agriculture et de l'alimentation
19 avenue du Maine - 75007 Paris – France
Tél.: 33/16 1 49 55 49 55

campaign for the promotion of landscapes and local produce: the "Paysages de Reconquête" seal of quality

Coopérative laitière de Beaufort – France

As a means of according national recognition to small regions which have directed their economic development towards quality, whether in terms of produce, environment, landscape or standards of hospitality, the Minister of the Environment decided in 1992 to attach the quality seal "Paysage de Reconquête" to about 100 regions.

The Beaufortain, in the Alps, was one of the regions thus distinguished for its success in holding out against the prevalent development models of twenty years ago and maintaining numerous farm holdings on a full-time basis or in combination with another activity, improving the quality of the Beaufort cheese to make it the best French gruyère, and placing the tourism emphasis on the quality of a living and well-kept landscape.

In 1993, a new requirement was added to the specification concerning the production of Beaufort cheese: not only is it to be made from the milk of cows of a certain race collected twice daily; it must in addition conform to the principle of fodder

autonomy, in other words the animals must have been given forage or foodstuffs produced inside the boundary to which the seal of quality applies, so providing a guarantee of good countryside stewardship. This idea, which is new to France, is an acknowledgement of the fact that the character of a locality comes out in the quality of its products and in the quality of the landscape.

Contact: Mr J. Cabanel
Ministry of the Environment - Landscape Office
20, avenue de Se'gur - 75007 Paris - France
Phone: 33/16 1 42 19 18 81

revival of red pepper production

Paprika, originally grown in America, made its way to the great Hungarian plain in the 17th century, finding a favourable sunny habitat in the vicinity of the town of Kalocsa. It took the expertise, hard labour and patience of many generations to develop the seasoning paprika, bright red in colour, with a piquant taste and permanent high quality from what was originally a very hot spice. Paprika is not only used for flavouring and colouring; it is also a rich source of elements essential for humans, including vitamins C, P, B1 and B2.

Arpad KAKONYL – Hungary

The large-scale production technology of the sixties significantly damaged the reputation of Hungarian paprika. To meet the requirements of the European market the Hungarians had to change the growing technology. The new species of high value ingredients require careful nurturing, with the emphasis on manual husbandry. This rules out the use of chemicals. The traditional manual harvest prevents damage to berries. Careful string or net-drying in front of houses guarantees the development of the colour.

Efforts in production and marketing are being made to revive traditional paprika growing, to stimulate the local economy using ancient know-how and to sustain the production of the "red-gold" paprika (the local gem).

Contact: Mr Arpald Kakonyi
Kiskunság National Park
Liszt F.19 H-6000 Kecskemet – Hungary
Phone: 36/76 482 611 – Fax: 36/76 481 074

. . . *accessible to all*

Access to the countryside is a right worth defending against appropriation
by a minority, for whatever purpose, be it pleasure,
(beaches, golf courses, private hunting grounds, etc.) or production alone,
with immense, impenetrable crop fields
and conifer forests at every bend in the road.

At a more general level, it is necessary to consider how the landscape should be
treated to suit each type of network:
civil engineering structures, highways, motorways,
service roads or rambling trails.
Thought must be given both to the functional aspects
of travel and to the idea of discovery
and the enjoyment to be derived by local inhabitants and tourists alike from walking
and travelling.

High-speed travel has engendered a new way of perceiving landscapes.
Views come into sight more suddenly
and sensations are simplified. No single view, whether it be that of the motorway
traveller or of the high-speed train passenger, should take precedence
over the view which the inhabitants have of the landscape.

A better course and a more enriching one would be to call forth the sensations felt by the walker, the cyclist or the herdsman,
to work with the grain and the principal threads that structure the landscape.
Seen from the motorway, the great plain of the Beauce
in the Paris basin can stir up strong emotions on account of its immensity and the sky above it, but from the walker's point of view,
if there are no more footpaths, there is no way of penetrating this landscape and experiencing it from within.

How to design these networks is a matter that must be considered at a very early stage when discussing the future of the countryside.

some lines of action

◆ Maintaining, protecting and developing networks of ecologically acceptable roads and footpaths in the countryside.

◆ Promoting highway embellishment policies.

◆ Introducing landscape awareness into the design and construction of all infrastructures.

Upgrade the hydroelectric dam

Upgrade the built heritage: village, factory, sawmill, open-air museum, bridge, etc. (Local authority, voluntary organisations, industry)

Restore the visual connections along and across the valley: land clearance, drainage. (Local authority, landowners, farmers, electricity board, forest managers)

Open and upgrade the landscape as seen from the road through broadleaved tree alignment. Improve the legibility of crossroads

F. BONNEAUD . V. BRUNET [paysagistes DPLG.

The vallée de la Plaine landscape scheme

landscape plans: the example of the Vallée de la Plaine in the Vosges

A Landscape Plan is not an extra conservation document, nor is it a new procedure or even what is commonly called a landscape design study.

It is a dynamic process, bringing together all those who help to make the landscape and those who benefit from it. The objective of this new approach is to stimulate debate about the landscape within the locality from a description of the assets it possesses, the constraints it is under and the points at issue within it, so that the scheme which finally emerges is one that has been discussed and accepted by all.

The population of the Vallee de la Plaine in the Vosges has been declining very rapidly over the past forty years with the departure of the textile mill and its workers, who also looked after the meadows bordering the river. The sombre rows of spruce subsequently planted on these meadows shroud the village in darkness, creating such an unattractive atmosphere that the few remaining inhabitants almost lost heart.

"Give our valley back its light" is now the slogan which unites elected representatives, farmers, foresters, landowners, inhabitants and engineers specialising in highway construction, water supply, electricity networks and telephone communications in their endeavour to clear the ground and beautify the landscape, each at his own level and within his own territory. All work is carried out on a contract basis. None of the basic instruments required by law (land-use plans, tree planting regulations, etc.) is put to use until a wide-ranging debate on objectives has taken place. Photographs, drawings and group rambles are the chief means by which a collective project is put together, the richness of the region rediscovered and hope restored.*

Contact: Mr Marc Verdier C.A.U.E. des Vosges
5, rue Gambetta - 88000 Epinal – France
Phone: 33/29 33 89 40

observance of democratic procedures

Everyone helps to fashion the landscape, every day: farmers, highway engineers,
bricklayers, architects, foresters, local government representatives, officials drawing up
rules and regulations, local inhabitants, etc.
The result is disappointing when the landscape thus created is simply an accumulation
of effects produced individually on the physical
environment without prior consultation or planning;
for it means that each technique is merely self-serving and that the overall outcome,
the new landscape, is simply rather disorderly
and the consequence of incoherent sectoral approaches made
independently of one another.

The other way of making the landscape is to regard it as a collective project
involving everyone.
In this way, no technique claims supremacy but is put to use
in the common cause.
This social project is the concerted result of a shared approach.
Those involved must think about the desired landscape and find ways of weighing up
and comparing all individual constraints and aspirations.
Through discussion and exchange of ideas,
the partners can reach a consensus formalised by quality charters,
conventions and contracts.

This approach requires that the views of the community be heard and the services of all relevant experts enlisted: historians, geographers, geologists, landscape designers, town planners, naturalists, etc.
Artists have a role here, too, to formalise the transition from discussing how the system (ecological, agronomic, economic) should operate to envisaging the form and structure (landscape) that this system will adopt, and to sketch new utopias.

In order to make the landscape the expression of a social project, consideration must be given to the methods that will facilitate the coming together of different points of view.

some lines of action

◆ Developing landscape plans, contracts and charters.

◆ Channelling skills and sensitivities into landscape planning.

◆ Developing training in landscape design and making technicians and scientists sensitive to aesthetic and artistic considerations.

◆ Fostering community involvement.

Centre méditerranéen de l'environnement – France.

the European Environment Study Groups

A European programme to support local landscape improvement initiatives.

The European Environment Study Groups are workshops which have been operating on the ground for the past four years with the support of the European Union, enabling students in the environmental disciplines to make a voluntary contribution to numerous landscape improvement projects:

In the Algarve (Portugal) an inventory of landscape units was compiled prior to the creation of an open-air museum.

In the region of Apulia (Italy) a plan for the protection and enhancement of dry stone constructions (trulli) was drawn up.

In the Vaucluse (France) a preliminary study was made concerning the management of windbreak hedges.

In London (United Kingdom) the group helped to prepare a scheme for a park on a vacant industrial site.

In the programme for 1994, the European Environment Study Groups give priority to landscaping in the vicinity of historic monuments.

Contact: Mr Jean-Baptiste Lanaspèze
Groupement Européen des Campus de l'Environnement
41, cours Jean-Jaures - 84000 Avignon – France
Phone: 33/90 27 08 61

postscript

In 1348 in Tuscany, in a period racked by wars between the Italian republics, when the landscape had been ravaged by flood and erosion and the population decimated by the Great Plague, Ambrogio Lorenzetti depicted his view of the ideal landscape in his *Allegory of Good Government* wall decoration in the Council Chamber in Siena. His vision gives equal value to the town and the countryside, is inspired by the agronomic and architectural inventions of his day, reflects the social aspiration to "harmony" and expresses the values of humanism.

This "beautiful landscape" of his imagination, at the time still an unattained ideal, later became reality, and is still very like the landscapes that we can admire today in the countryside around Siena.

The monks of the Middle Ages, the artists of the Renaissance, the seventeenth-century English agronomists who invented the hedgerow landscape, the Dutch engineers of the eighteenth century who succeeded in draining lakes and marshes all over Europe, the French schools of *Ponts et Chaussées* and *Arts et Métiers* where the idea of engineering design originated, all combined art, science and a love of mankind and all living things in everything they undertook. With the peasants, foresters and craftsmen of the countryside as their associates, they were Europe's great landscape designers.

In this line of descent, new relationships must be devised between town and country, north and south, east and west.

We must preserve this culture, this openness of mind, this ability to dream and this rapport with the earth and with nature, so that we may savour the enjoyment of being involved in shaping tomorrow's landscapes.

appendix

Recommendation No. R (94) 6 of the Committee of Ministers to member states for a sustainable development and use of the countryside.

with a particular focus on the safeguarding of wildlife and landscapes

(Adopted by the Committee of Ministers on 5 September 1994 at the 516th meeting of the Ministers' Deputies)

The Committee of Ministers, in pursuance of Article 15.*b* of the Statute of the Council of Europe,

1. Having regard to the work done by the Council of Europe for the countryside, the work undertaken by other international organisations, the Declaration of the Ministerial Conference "An Environment for Europe" (Lucerne, 1993) and that of the International Conference on "Conserving Europe's Natural Heritage: towards a European Ecological Network" (Maastricht, 1993);

2. Having regard to the requirements of the Convention on the Conservation of European Wildlife and Natural Habitats (Bern Convention), of Recommendation No. 25 on the conservation of natural areas outside protected areas proper and of the European Conservation Strategy;

3. Aware that the countryside covers the greater part of European territory, in which a large proportion of the population resides;

4. Recognising that rural communities have played, and will continue to play, a significant role in the preservation of the cultural heritage and the management of natural resources, particularly soil, water, air, flora and fauna;

5. Aware that the countryside contains a very large proportion of Europe's rich landscape assets and the majority of its natural and semi-natural habitats, which are of great value to the conservation of our natural heritage;

6. Recognising that rural landscapes are illustrations of the age-old relationship between man and his environment;

7. Aware that the future of the countryside is now under threat from the two divergent and contradictory paths along which rural areas are rapidly moving; on the one hand some regions are at risk of depopulation, while on the other hand there are regions threatened by intensive use for agriculture or forestry, urban expansion, industrialisation, infrastructure developments or increased pressure of tourism, sport and recreation;

8. Aware that, whichever of these two extremes rural areas are moving towards, the results are a loss of cultural identity, severe socio-economic problems and major difficulties in terms of the protection and management of the environment and landscape;

9. Defining the sustainable development of the countryside as the long-term improvement of the population's living conditions, which implies a comprehensive, concerted and coherent approach to ecological, cultural, social and economic requirements, and signifies that priority must be accorded – at all levels and at all times – to maintaining the countryside's production capacity and assets in the long term, and to making sustainable development objectives consistent with the demands;

10. Particularly recognising the human race's role in maintaining this balance, since, on the one hand, it must continue its positive action to preserve the quality and richness of the landscapes it has shaped, while, on the other hand, it must moderate the scope of its action in order to avoid any deterioration of rural landscapes and/or cultural heritage;

11. Recognising that the extent of the present crisis affecting the countryside and its interaction with macro-economic processes require the implementation of a common and integrated approach for a sustainable development and use of the countryside;

12. Recognising that the diversity of local situations means that such an approach needs to be implemented through policies and action harmonised at local, regional, national and international level and appropriate to the potential and limits of natural habitats;

13. Recognising that adherence to the principles of sustainable rural development requires the safeguarding, management, rehabilitation and, wherever appropriate, creation of quality rural landscapes and the imparting of information and of a sense of responsibility to all policy-makers;

14. Recognising that these objectives can be achieved only with the committed involvement of all sections of the sections of the population in a community made up of aware, adequately informed and responsible individuals;

Recommends that governments of member States, in establishing their policy for the countryside, give special attention to the conservation of wildlife and landscapes, and to this end, base their policy on the principles and measures set out in appendix to this recommendation.

Appendix to Recommendation No. R (94) 6

Principles and measures
for a sustainable development and use of the countryside

I. A comprehensive, concerted and coherent approach to sustainable rural development

1. Ensure that the aims of nature and landscape conservation are promoted by statutory, regulatory, administrative and financial measures and avoid any measures that might work against them, such as inappropriate public assistance, inadequate or over-strict technical standards.

2. Encourage a change in the methods of economic calculation and analysis, which are all too often confined to the profitability of production units, taking no account of the costs of a preserved nature, the costs of harm done to nature and the environment and the costs of restoring the enviroment borne by the state or by individuals.

3. Ensure that not only the many traditional functions of agriculture, stock farming and forestry, but also their new roles of countryside management, cultural heritage preservation, protection of natural resources and wildlife conservation are both enhanced and taken into account in all sectoral policies.

4. Start a process of periodic monitoring and reassessment of sustainable development policies in the light of the desired objectives.

II. Harmonisation at regional level of human activities with the potential and limits of natural habitats

1. Draw up spatial planning rules which take account of the preconditions for ecological balance, such as soil and water conservation, measures to neutralise and prevent the spread of pollutants, and action to safeguard the natural assets of the countryside and its value in landscape terms.

2. Make it compulsory to assess the environmental impact using recognised methods, and to carry out follow-up monitoring of intensive production systems given the physical, chemical, biological and socio-economic impacts, and devise rules to reduce their adverse effects on the countryside.

3. Ensure the sustainable use of the resources required for agriculture, forestry and fisheries and guarantee soil fertility and the appropriate management of water resources.

4. Take care to maintain varied activities complementary to agriculture and forestry, guaranteeing long-term viability, balance and socio-economic stability, such as rural tourism, recreation and leisure, hunting and any crafts, industries or services which do not affect the natural and cultural heritage adversely.

5. Safeguard and increase diversity in the choice of crop types and natural, ancient or local breeds and methods of stock-rearing for their potential to contribute to respect for the environment.

6. Structure landscapes in order to stimulate natural processes of self-purification and revitalisation, limit the concentration of pollutants and their spread into natural habitats and control non-specific sources of pollution, especially through simple and inexpensive means such as windbreaks, hedgerows, natural meadows, ponds and buffer zones.

7. Promote and intensify agronomic research, through pilot projects, for example, with a view to implementing new agronomic systems for integrated production and organic farming which respect the natural balance and the ecological load capacity of each region.

8. Safeguard rural community skills in harmony with modern techniques.

III. Creation and management of quality rural landscapes

1. Compile inventories, or use existing ones, of landscape types in order better to understand, among other things, the development of landscapes and of the man-made and natural constituent elements of each unit, such as natural meadows, wetlands, woods and thickets, hedgerows and bocage, orchards and single trees, terraces and dry-stone walls, stone crosses, rock-cut monuments and other features of value. These data should be readily accessible to those persons who wish to make use of them.

2. Develop appropriate tools for the protection and management of landscapes which are exceptional for their natural, aesthetic, cultural or historical value, their fragility or the pressures to which they are subjected.

3. Create ecological networks of natural and semi-natural habitats at all levels and related networks of structural landscape elements at local level, through measures designed to protect, restore, manage and create valuable natural and structural landscape elements, particularly those set out above.

4. Maintain footpaths and other rural rights of way as a means of access to the landscape so as to avoid, among other things, the proliferation of roads.

5. Devise and bring into general use a range of economic mechanisms and a variety of regulations and incentives, at both national and international level, such as:

   a. ecological management on a contractual basis between farmers, landowners, governments and/or voluntary organisations, with provision for financial remuneration or compensation;

   b. economic and fiscal measures such as land tax abatement or exemption, charges on polluting phytosanitary products, offers of subsidies and loans, etc.;

   c. opportunities for organisations, be they governmental or non-governmental, to purchase sites if they are interested in so doing;

   d. regulations restricting the use of chemicals and/or potentially polluting agricultural practices, principally in sensitive areas;

   e. planning instruments such as green belt or landscape schemes;

   f. action to improve the image and sales potential of environmentally benign products;

   g. market mechanism adjustments on behalf of rural areas, taking account of their specific needs;

h. environmentally friendly measures to encourage farmers in areas where agriculture alone cannot provide a livelihood to diversify their activity;

i. development and creation of appropriate training infrastructures to train local people to acquire the necessary new skills.

IV. Harmonisation of action and policies at all levels of authority

1. Draw up regional development policy schemes which take account of coherent territorial entities based on natural conditions, socio-economic and cultural situations as well as the state of the environment.

2. Ensure, out of a concern for the principles of democracy, justice and solidarity between citizens, and with a view to safeguarding the natural heritage, that all regions have at their disposal resources appropriate to their needs, if necessary by transferring resources from the wealthiest to the most disadvantaged regions.

3. Apply, wherever appropriate, the subsidiarity principle by delegating responsibility for defining and applying measures to foster sustainable rural development to the lowest competent level of authority, the one closest to those actively involved in rural community life.

V. Community involvement and training

1. Inform and convince all sections of society that sustainable development of the countryside is indispensable to human health as well as to the quality of the environment and life in general.

2. Convey to those who use the countryside, many of whom are town dwellers, that it is not possible to demand quality landscapes and at the same time retain lifestyles and consumption habits that cause deterioration of the environment.

3. Inform, alert and educate members of the public about landscape and environmental protection and endeavour to make them change their behaviour by showing them that they share responsibility and have scope to take action.

4. Set up facilities and schemes whereby people can seek education and advice, exchanging information and comparing their experience, and make training courses available, so that the new ways of facilitating changes in the countryside can be publicised rapidly.

5. Rally not only people from the countryside but the public as a whole, in a design for society dedicated to landscapes and nature conservation.

In the same series:

1. Hedges, (1988) ISBN 92-871-1555-9
2. Farming and wildlife (1989) ISBN 92-871-1685-7
3. Watercourses. Conservation, maintenance and management (1994) ISBN 92-871-1894-9